MW01204465

The Spiral Affect
Jacqueline James

PUBLISHED *by* PARABLES
Earthly Stories with a Heavenly Meaning

ISBN 978-1-945698-66-8

Printed in the United States of America

The Spiral Affect
Jacqueline James

PUBLISHED *by* PARABLES
Earthly Stories with a Heavenly Meaning

Table of Content.

Entertainment
1. Open Mic
2. Print This
3. Nothin Comin
4. The Movement
5. Out There
6. Beautiful Sky
7. Stinky
8. The Neighbor
9. I Write
10. Do it
11. Wild Stallion

Special Dedication
1. T. D.
2. Baby Boy
3. The Message
4. Faith
5. Blessed
6. Praise God
7. Loyal Days
8. Comfort

About the Author

Jacqueline James is a highly devoted Christian author. She's well recognized throughout her community for her humble spirit and unique style of writing. She brings clarity to the art of the spoken words, by gently expressing them, through her prestigious talent. She's well known and appreciated for her contributions to her church, family, friends, and everyone she can be of assistance to. Jacqueline has sparked the nation with her first intriguing book, 'Poetry with a Twist,' a best seller, in record-breaking time.

God has blessed Jacqueline with an epiphany, which gave her the perseverance to compose countless poems expressed through her spirituality. Her candid nature has uplifted, inspired, motivated, as well as influenced so many lives from every race, creed, color, and ethnicity. Jacqueline has broken down a wall of silence, creating a bridge to mends hearts, and unite families through her work.

The Dedication

This book is dedicated to my daughter Sherece Gecelle Whitehorn. Sherece is my first-born child, whom I greatly admire, for her ambition, and the dedication she has shown over the years to pursue her career. She has overcome many obstacles, as a single mother, and managed to obtain three degrees in different fields. Sherece also works diligently, to support herself and her children. She is well-rounded, and a respected woman in her area of expertise. Because Sherece and myself are so close in age, we've formed a unique mother/daughter relationship; she's not only my daughter, she's my friend. Over the years she's been a very important support system, by keeping me up to speed with the millennium changes and the world of technology.

Thank you Sherece for all you do, and I'm sure that you will continue to be an incredible mother because you're such an amazing person and a wonderful daughter.

Thank You

Special thanks go out to all the people who have helped me throughout the process of writing and publishing this book. First, I would like to say thank you mama, Jeannette Whitehorn, for your unconditional love, and always being my biggest fan!

I also would like to send a special thanks to my darling cousin Felicia Holyfield, who always made time for me, through her busy schedule, to listen with a kind ear, hear with an open heart, and critique with a professional view. I appreciate all that you've done, and please continue.

Also, I would like to thank my daughter Jeannie Davis and my sons Cedric Haynes, and Centilus Buchanan, for their help, love, support, and most of all their patience with me, during this amazing journey.

Thank you to my son Charles Buchanan, for his support, encouragement, and for allowing me to share my poems with his friends.

I want to thank Sandra Alexander, for answering the phone "in the wee morning" or middle of the night and allowing me to read her a bedtime story. Thanks, friend!

I appreciate Janice Johnson, for her support, good company, and lots of laughs.

A special thanks to my cousin Monica Admas, for her love and time.

I would also like to thank my publisher Dr. John Dee Jefferies from *Publishing by Parables,* for working diligently with me doing this process, and for becoming a friend.

This book couldn't be possible without the help from all my friends at Office Depot in Bridgeton, Missouri, who gracefully named me Ms. Poem, and were always there to kindly assist me.

Additionally, I want to thank my church family at Nazareth Temple presiding, Bishop Melvin Smith and First Lady Jacqueline Smith, for all their love, support, and encouragement during my Christian walk.

But most importantly, I thank God, for the peace He's blessed me with, to continue to write countless poems, with each one of them, reflecting his beauty within me.

Thank you, Jesus!

Introduction

This is a book of carefully selected, marvelously written poems, created by the well-known, and respected Christian author, Jacqueline James. Through her unique, and diverse style of writing, she has composed some beautiful and original, poems filled with passion. Jacqueline spent countless hours with the intention to entertain, intrigue, inspire, and educate her audience. This book is guaranteed to satisfy your thirst for the art of poetry.

This book is meant to inform you of some general aspects of life. It will entertain you in a very pleasing, and authentic way. It will also educate you on various unaddressed issues, and inspire you spiritually. All while soothing you into a comfortable position to accept primary life endeavors. Jacqueline has creatively composed all these aspects into this book of poetry. She intends to leave a memorable impression on all her readers. Jacqueline has used her fundamental skills to captivate her audience, in a vibrant and inspiring manner. Her efforts are to please your sense of awareness, through the pleasure of poetry.

Chapter 1

General

Raillery...

To have an absolute intangible relationship with a stranger is
obscured;
Scavenging through endless possibilities of deceit;
Grasping for each truth untold;
There's no admittance of indiscretion;
They present themselves with a union;
One can easily be distracted with raillery and manipulation.

Pain...

Throbbing, aching, torturous, feeling, I'm about to go insane;
Hopelessly, miserable from this pain:
Continuously hurting and dreadfully sad;
Helplessly overwhelmed, I'm about to go mad:
Laying around feeling tired and lazy;
It hurts so bad I'm about to go crazy:
Taking medicine and pills just for some relief;
In spite of my faith, and all of my beliefs:
It hurts, it hurts, and it hurts a lot;
I'm sore all over, without a doubt:
I'm hurting everywhere from my condition;
I only get temporary relief from my physician:
The stuff I'm going through has no cure;
The pain grows stronger every year;
It's bad, it's horrible that's for certain;
I want to scream and shout cause I'm hurting:
Stab me, shake me, beat me up;
I know about pain, I know what's up!
Piercing intensely, while I'm in motion;
Searching desperately for a healing potion,
The pain is hovering all over me;
I want desperately for it to flee:
Continued On Next Page

I can't function, I can't think;
It had me incapacitated, for over a week:
This pain is sharp, achy, and very hard;
I can't get comfortable or drop my guard:
I've always tried to play it off;
I don't complain or open my mouth:
But now it's becoming too severe;
It's going to last forever; I'm starting to fear,
I accept it all because it lives in me;
However, I pray for mercy, to set it free.
:

No Joy...

You've been so bitter and mean all your life;
No wonder no man never made you his wife:
You always walked around as if you were in control;
You never try to hide it; you were arrogant and bold:
You ruined so many lives, with that poison you spread;
You stepped on so many people, just for you to get ahead:
It's not by chance the predicament you're in;
Left alone without any friends:
You ran everybody away, and didn't allow them to get close;
You thought you were "high-saditty," and meant the most:
I'm not judging you; I'm just stating the facts;
How you were so obnoxious and blamed it on the next:
You never took any responsibilities, for all that crap that you did;
You kept it bottled up in a jar, with a tight lid:
You need to admit what you did, to the people you hurt;
So, they can find closure, after you desert:
You have no JOY only guilt and shame;
Even though your mother gave you, that name:
The time has come to face your demons;
Ask God for forgiveness, during this holiday season.

Chapter 2

Spiritual

1. Peace
2. The healer
3. Hope
4. Praying for healing

Peace...

Our congregation joins together to worship and pray;
For spiritual healing, throughout the day:
When we come together and fellowship;
We can feel the joy, as our hearts lift:
As we meet during each week for several hours;
We all revive our Holy Ghost power:
We share a church family connection;
As the spirit moves us, in a righteous direction:
We continue a spiritual journey, throughout our life;
In order to grow closer to our Lord and Savior, Jesus Christ:
When our lives take us through difficult and challenging times;
God is a comforter, for both yours and mine:
He doesn't want us to have pain or hidden scars;
He wants us to use him diligently, that's what he died for:
(Mathew 6:11)

Jesus said, "Peace be unto you."
Our Father's words are true:
All he asks is for us to believe;
And all our burdens will be relieved:
Faith is what it's all about;
Knowing Jesus is love, we won't be without:
Come on and pray, and trust Jesus for yourself;
I can guarantee, you'll never need anyone else:
(Mathew 7:7)

"Ask, and it shall be given unto you; seek and ye shall find; knock,
and it shall be opened unto you:"
All of Jesus words are true;
Give your life to God; he'll see you through:
As we share our story;
To God be the glory!

The Healer...

My niece is sick, but she's very brave;
Chemo treatment is how she spends her day:
She's very sweet, and wise as well;
This will not beat her, I can definitely tell:
The illness she has doesn't discriminate;
From Whites, Blacks, Chinese, Mexicans or any race:
Her recovery depends on a lot of dedication;
Her parents, family, and doctors are working in close relations:
There are a lot of resources available to her;
There are people throughout the community that really care:
There are lots of children in the same situation;
Their parents are in need of some confirmation:
They all need to know that their child's okay;
And gain some perspective on the results, at the end of the day:
This whole process is new to us all;
But, her doctors assure us, they'll always be on call:
However, God is a healer, and we know this to be true;
We trust in his mercy, to bring her through:
Through the power of prayer, she'll be alright;
We won't give in to this sickness; we'll continue to fight:
Both of her parents wish they could trade places,
and take her pain away;
To God be the Glory, to bring her brighter days:

God is healing her body, as we speak;
She's laughing and playing and doesn't feel weak:
He's giving her joy, in the midst of the storm;
No weapon against her, shall ever form:
Her load lightened because God was on call;
The prayers and praises came from us all:
We thank you, Jesus, in advance;
We give you Glory, as we lift our hands.

Hope...

Lost souls are looking for hope in a bottle;
The savior delivers at any hour:
The pain will cause you to do drugs and drink;
The depression becomes so strong; you can't focus or think;
Expecting satisfaction from anywhere;
Never allowing yourself to care:
Desiring the best from your life;
However, refusing the challenges, from the fight:
So, when you're desperate, and in need of relief;
There's spiritual healing, in your beliefs:
You won't need to search, or look too far;
God will deliver you from wherever you are:
Accept Jesus in your heart; he'll give you hope;
Without alcohol, drugs or any dope:
You can always expect miracles to happen;
When you're not sailing your ship, but God is the captain:
When your struggle in life seems to get harder;
Put your faith in the One that troubles the water:
When you're getting desperate and starting to doubt;
Hope is the results of Jesus bringing you out:
Put God first in everything that you say and do;
And you'll feel his anointing delivering you:
He'll grant you peace, surpassing all understanding;
If you hide His Word in your heart and keep His commandments.

Praying For Healing...

Please Lord hear our cry;
Thank you, Jesus;
We come before you, humbling ourselves;
Thank you, Jesus;
Our Faith is in you Lord;
We trust you Lord with all our hearts;
Thank you, Jesus;
A prayer for the sick, old, and young:
Please, Lord, bless from the crown of their head;
To the soles of their feet, and everything in between:
Thank you, Jesus;
Isaiah 53:5 says "through your stripes we are healed;"
Heal their body, Lord;
We ask in Jesus name with all our hearts:
Thank you, Jesus;
Jesus, you died on Calvary and shed your blood;
To save your people, with your love:
Thank you, Jesus;
Bless them, Jesus;
Show them you died for this very reason;
Thank you, Jesus;
Cure their sickness Lord, and relieve their pain;
We believe it's done in Jesus name:
Thank you, Jesus;

We thank you Lord Jesus for all the things you're about to do;
Heal their body Lord and bring them through:
Thank you, Jesus;
God this is not a selfish prayer;
You promise not to give them more than they could bare:
Thank you, Jesus;
We love you Jesus, may your- will- be- done;
To heal the sick, old, and the young:
Thank you, Jesus;
Lord, you said if two or more touch and agree in your name, your
word wouldn't come back void:
We're praying in agreement Lord.
And we're praying hard:
Thank you, Jesus;
God in your word you said if two or more gather in your name,
you will be in the mist of it all;
It's us Lord, the sheep of your flock;
Wanting mercy and favor, Lord you are our Rock:
Thank you, Jesus;
Please, Jesus, turn this situation around;
Heal their body, from their feet to their crown:
Thank you, Jesus;
Bless them, Lord, hold them safe in your arms;
Keep them, Lord, no weapon formed against them can do her no
harm:
Thank you, Jesus;
Please Lord have mercy;
Lord, please have mercy;
Thank you, Jesus;
Mercy Lord;
Thank you, Jesus;
Mercy Lord;
Thank you, Jesus;
Thank you, Jesus, for your mercy;
Thank you, Jesus, for your healing;
Thank you, Jesus, for your blood;
Thank you, Jesus, for your love;

Thank you, Jesus, for your blessings;
Thank you, Jesus, for your amazing grace;
Thank you, Jesus, for hearing our cry Lord;
Thank you, Jesus, for relieving their pain Lord;
Thank you, Jesus, for turning this situation around Lord;
Thank you, Jesus, for favor Lord;
Thank you, Jesus, for being our comforter in our darkest hour
Lord;
Thank you, Jesus, for being a doctor in our sick-room Lord;
Thank you for being our rock;
Thank you, Jesus, for all you've done Lord;
Thank you, Jesus, for all you're about to do Lord;
Thank you, Jesus;
Thank you, Jesus;
All these things we ask and believe in Jesus name we pray;
Thank you, Jesus,
Amen

Chapter 3

Educational

1. Dr. Martin Luther King Jr.
2. Teach them
3. Past...Present...Future.
4. To your dreams
5. He had a dream

Dr. Martin Luther King Jr...

Thank you, Jesus, for loaning us your angel of peace;
He was truly non-violent until his decease;
Today we lift our voice to sing;
Happy Birthday Dr. Martin Luther King:
He was taken from this world too soon;
But not before he was able to share his news:
All the things he did and said were right;
He was non-violent, and refuse to fight:
All his love and peace changed the world;
It opened doors for many boys and girls;
Because he tried to live without any sin;
It made people scared of the things he did:
He walked, and walked for many miles;
And those who followed respected his style:
He paved the way for many generations to come;
And when it was done our freedom was won,
He got word to the president;
And laws started to change when it was sent:
A lot of his followers was trampled on, beaten, and, bruised;
Because of the 'WHITE MAN' laws that they refused:
Today we lift our voices to celebrate;
The legacy he left for all our race.
Happy Birthday Dr. Martin Luther King.
Together we stand, and together we sing!

Teach them…

They're just messing with the black kid's education;
Saying that the parents or not quite dedicated;
They need to find better jobs to get more money,
to buy better homes;
So, their kids could live in better school zones:
We need to wake up and turn this stuff around;
To make sure they don't keep on dumbing our kid's down:
And if you think I'm preaching the same sad song;
Then why are your kids being left home alone:
Raise your kids, show them love, and give them discipline;
So, they don't end up on welfare, or in the prison system:
Stop letting your kids wear what they want, say what they want,
and do what they want to do;

Make them responsible and accountable too:
When you're at home, you think it's cute when
'Little Johnny' says a bad word;
But when he says it in public, you act as
if it's something you never heard:
Teach them that home training, starts at home;
Let them stay kids, while they're kids;
They'll have the rest of their life's to be grown:
It's not cute, watching them mock you;
And you wonder why they grew up, confused,
not knowing what to do:

Because their minds weren't mature enough,
for the things that they went through:
And if you're one of those parents, then shame on you:
And if you don't teach them right from wrong;
The street will show them when they leave your home:
Ok, in most homes there's only one parent in the house, but, "best
believe," the kids, or not the boss:
The problem is you worried about hurting
'Little Johnny's' feelings;
When you don't have no money or nothing to give him:
Now he's walking around thinking the world owes him something;
But if you don't get it together, he's going to end up with nothing;
You're enabling him, from becoming the man, he needs to be;
And it's pissing off mothers, like me:
We must challenge their energy, and teach them respect;
Our children are highly intelligent, and that's a fact;
We must prepare them, to be wise,
and strong for when they get older;
Because the weight of the world, is on their shoulder:
Don't tell me, all of this is coming to you as a surprise;
Because the "WHITE MAN" is out planning a mass genocide:
Educate your kids, my people of color;
You're their father, and their mother:
Our children will be destined for great things;
If we just invest the time and stop encouraging sin:
Parents don't allow your children to party with you;
Give them something age appropriate, to do:
Enroll them in sports, or some sort of activity;
Make sure that they get exercise and plenty:
Keep them off social media's;
Our kids need us to talk and read to them:
Allow them to express themselves through play;
And don't forget to give them chores to do, each day:
Start by teaching them spiritual awareness,
and giving them spiritual guidance;
They'll grow up as Christians without defiance:

Show interest in your children work,
and the things that they're interested in;
Be their parent and the leader and stop trying to be their friend:
Teach them how to respect themselves, by respecting them first:
Don't drink or indulge in their presence,
and always showing them the worse;
Give them something to look forward to, from the
accomplishments, that they've achieved;
Teach them about God's grace, and make sure that they believe:
Keep them inspired, to always do positive things;
Help them to understand the blessing that God brings:
Bring your children to Christ, because he only loaned them to you;
Have faith in his love to see them through:
Now that I've shared with you the best way,
to turn this situation around;
Put your best effort forward, and do it now:
Save the children from themselves;
And this will also be saving yourself:
Just a little advice, to put in place;
People of color save your race.

Past...Present...Future...

These are some of our great minds
Through the early centuries of time:
These are stories from our present;
Through our people of color, we measure:
These are prayers for our future;
In the hope that our generation doesn't remain neutral:
In our praise we need to sing;
Through God's grace our faith we bring;
Our ancestors where inventors, activist, doctors, and lawyers;
Our children shall once again achieve it all,
through the Holy Ghost power:
We study our past, to understand and appreciate our present;
We acknowledge our presence to inspire and enhance our future
with no measure.

Our forefathers were scientists, poets, artists, and athletes:
They were intelligent and loyal and some of the humblest
people to meet:
We educate our youth so they'll appreciate the
blood that's flowing through their veins;
That they're destined for great things, and society will also
remember their names:
We're living through history as we speak;
Our black people are teachers, politicians,
gourmet chefs, and even priests:

We had a black president for two terms, and that's a miracle itself;
We have bishops, astronauts, firefighters,
a whole lot of other greatness left:
We've come a long way, and we have a long way to come as well;
There are stories about great conquerors, Civil Right Activist
and Men of Honor to tell:
The things our people of color have accomplished
were marvelous and great;
The present generations can successfully achieve
as well, without debate:
Work hard, and be loyal wherever your place;
You'll find comfort through prayer, from God's love and grace:
(Philippians 4:13)
We can do all things through Christ who strengthen us:
Through faith in Jesus, we put our trust.

To Your Dreams...

Children, children, children I am speaking to you;
You can become whatever you decide to be;
You have your future inside of you,
follow your heart to your destiny:
Don't allow disappointments to make you discouraged;
Have faith in Jesus; he'll keep you encouraged:
Follow your dreams, even if it means reaching past
the stars in the sky;
With perseverance, and passion, show endurance until you die:
Never give up, push through with all your strength;
Show the world that you are a Christian,
and that makes you relentless:
Learn from your ancestor's pass, and their accomplishments
through life;
Invoke knowledge from their spirit, to enrich your life:
Give it all you got, and all you got to give,
With resilience, and persistence, an honorable life you'll live:
Put God first in everything you say and do;
Trust in Jesus' love, to see you through;
Yes, your parents will be there to help guide you along the way;
But you must stand on your own and become accountable one day:
So, make wise decisions from the start;
Keep prayer in your life, praise in your day,
and Jesus in your heart!

He Had A Dream...

He did not dream, that one day our son's pants would be sagging;
Or that they'll be going around disrespecting
each other and continuously bragging.
Well, he dreamed one day we'll be free;
Free to self-destruct, I know that's not what he means:
Look around how many decent black men are left;
We don't have to wait for the 'White Man' to kill us;
We're doing a good job destroying ourselves:
He marched and marched along with hundreds by his side;
He fought the good fight, for our children to have pride:
Some were killed, stomped down, brutally beaten,
and even put in jail;
For our children to be free and have stories through history to tell:
It cost him his life, taken way to soon;
Just to win freedom that afternoon:
He paved the way for all generations to come;
Are there any loyal black men to carry on his legacy? Maybe none.
I challenge you, my black brothers,
I dare you to stand up for what's right;
And fight diligently even if it costs you your life:
To my sisters stand by your black man;
Give him love and support and help him to understand.

Mothers teach your babies before they come out of your womb;
Their ancestors where Kings and Queens, that wore silk and gold
costumes and are buried in ancient tombs:
We're descendant from warrior's,
fighting lions and tigers to survive;
Yet we're over here in America, and
can't conquer the "White Man's" lies:
Of course, there's some of us who are rich and living the
"American dream,"
To what expense did they pay, to watch their heritage
die, between the seams:
Ok, they donate a recreation center, feed the needy, and give to a
charity here and there;
To convince society that they really care;
But are they interacting, protesting the laws,
that help 'dumb' our children down;
So, they won't rise up to become leaders,
and once again wear that crown?
I'm not mad, nor do I have an attitude;
Don't get it twisted; it's not you I'm trying to impress;
I just have a message, that needs to be expressed:
Now you can draw your conclusions from the rest;
So, listen carefully, if your hearts pass the test:
You'll wake up one morning and look around, to find there's no-
one else in this world like you:
And you're being left alone, wondering what to do:

The 'White Man's planning a mass genocide;
They're eliminating an entire race, before their very own eyes:
They put the drugs in the man's hands;
So, he'll feel powerful over his domain:
Now he's selling the poison to his friends,
their wives, and their kids:
Once he makes progress from cash flow;
The police come around just to bust him down,
and off to jail he goes:
So, they give the woman "housing" for her and kids;

Under one condition, she can't let that man back in:
Now she's 'head-of-house-hold,' making all the decisions:
Working hard, taking care of the kids,
and sending money to the prison:
Daddy's in jail, mama's working late, the kids raising themselves;
Without discipline, no structure,
just street gangs, drugs, violence, and despair;
Jail or death? What's left?
It takes a man, to raise a boy into a man;
The streets don't care less if he was sagging his pants:
They're trying desperately to fit in, but they're lost;
But your daughter's bearing their babies will pay the cost:
Now the cycle continues, in one big circle of confusion;
But I'm here to give you the conclusion:
And I'll also give you the solution;

Put prayer back in our homes;
When men were marching strong:
We were once strong and united;
In the name of Jesus, we were fighting:
We're a strong race of people, and we marched without fear;
We need to exercise some resilience, and snap back into gear:
'He had a dream,' and it was meant for me and you:
Now we need to rise together and live it through.

Complete dedication to:
The late Dr. Martin Luther King Jr.

Chapter 4

Informative

Unpredictable...

Hot today, cold tomorrow;
Will I need a coat or just a sweater?
Nobody knows about this weather:
Will the sun rise high, or stay down low?
It's really, unpredictable:
If it's cold it's fine if it's hot it's okay;
I just want to know how to dress for the day:
Do I put on shorts, or do I wear long sleeves?
If I leave my jacket am I going to freeze?
I've seen people in slides, and some in boots;
If they catch a cold they'll have an excuse:
I put on a hat and started to sweat;
But when I took it off it wasn't warm enough yet:
I walk to my car and felt a chill;
By the time I got home I was feeling real ill:
My feet are hot; my hands are cold;
I even have a big red-nose:
Now I'm lying, in the bed don't want no cover;
Eating soup, and drinking hot tea- just trying to recover:
I stayed up late watching the news, trying to get the weather right;
But all their predictions change overnight:
I wear different outfits and a whole lot of clothes;

Am I going to need it all on? Nobody knows:
One wise woman once said "It's better to have it, and don't need
it, then to need it, and don't have it! "and another wise woman
said, "You can always take off, but you can't put on what you don't
have!"
Do I need to walk around with a laundry basket?
Just to make sure I'm staying in fashion:
It's an ice storm in the morning, sunshine in the afternoon; it's
raining in the evening;
And the snow's coming soon:
So, I don't need to guess how to dress in this mess;
I just put on some clothes and forget the rest:
Right now, is very critical;
Cause this weather is unpredictable!

Spirits...

Spirits,
They talked to me all day, and they talked to me all night;
They tell me what to say, and they give me what to write:
Some may call them 'ghost,' I'll call them my friends;
You'll find that they're harmless, if you allow them in:
They're always around me, they never really leave;
It's not like a magic trick, they're not in my hat, or up my sleeve:
Some call them angels watching over me;
I'll call them spirits, which you just can't see:
Some people call me 'schizo' others call me 'crazy';
I'm pretty sure I'm sane, and my thoughts are not hazy:
I hope they never leave because I enjoy their company;
When I follow their lead, they showed me that they're pleased:
You can believe it or not it doesn't really matter;
But if you get close enough, you can hear them chatter:
You can conjure them up, or you can just sit still;
They'll meet your presence if you have an open will.

Street Walkers...

They're all awake, they never sleep;
It's late at night; they need to freak:
They'll rob you, of all your earthly goods;
If this doesn't scare you, then it should:
They walk around in broad daylight;
Always trying to start a fight:
I have no idea what type of high that they're on;
The only thing that I know, is they like to roam:
It might be weed, or even crack;
I just know you better watch your back:
Some of them are drunk, others on pain pills;
They'll do whatever it takes, to get a cheap thrill:
They'll follow you around, and try to run some game;
Half of them or so delusional, they don't know their own name:
They have no ambitions, only attitude;
If you speak to them, they're very rude:
They'll laugh in your face like you're a big joke;
They're high off 'loud,' some type of smoke:
They have sex for money, to buy more drugs;
They're attracted only to sluts, and thugs:
They won't get jobs, to support themselves;
They rather steal from me, you, or anyone else:
They'll break into your homes, then try to justify it;
And the society sends them to rehab, to try and analyze them:

After weeks of therapy, professionals conclude;
That these 'streetwalkers' are just confused:
Some of them have very high IQs;
Which makes it easy to manipulate both me and you:
Some of them refuse to conform, to society ways;
They would rather live their life's as outcasts, walking around in a
daze:
Some are a bunch of incompetent peons;
That need to be locked away, in a cell or beyond:
Some of them may even become rehabilitated;
The others end up a bunch of people that are truly hated:
They spend their day going through an illusion;
Trying to get their next 'fix' is their solution:
They're always high, or drunk, they're never sober;
Their crap won't stop, into their lives are over.

The Fast...

We went through a fast, on a vegetarian diet;
I was eating all vegetables, and their varieties:
We had no meat products, not even cheese;
Use olive oil to fry, if you please:
No meat, no sweets those were the rules;
To eat successfully, I had to be schooled:
All our carbs products, where made from wheat;
Anything that didn't grow, we couldn't eat;
Our menu consists of all-natural foods;
When you change your diet, you change your mood:
It was a great sacrifice;
To give up my donut, cakes, and apple pies:
All the steaks, chicken, fish, and shrimp, I went without;
But when I gave up that pizza, I had to pout:
I ate things like broccoli, cauliflower, and asparagus;
When the 'fast,' was over I definitely weighed less:
We ate apples, oranges, bananas, and pears;
Strawberries, cantaloupes, and kiwis, if you dare;
We had mixed greens, carrots, squash, and other healthy foods;
I made lots of smoothies, and that was pretty cool:
I had a special delight, cooked in a tortilla shell;
It consists of smashed chili beans, baked with 'Rotel':
Continued On Next Page

I made a veggie special, vegetarian soup;
It had sweet peas, corn, green beans, kidney beans, lima beans,
potatoes, tomatoes, and noodles too:
We ate salads made with lettuce, sunflower seeds,
and a lot of different types of nuts;
I'm sure all these proteins, were good for our guts;
If you want to 'fast,' you must be willing to commit;
It was hard in the beginning, I must admit:
I really don't know how long this 'fast' is going to last;
Cause eating healthy, takes a whole lot of cash:
It has good benefits if you decide to try it;
It's 'The Daniels Fast' the 21-day diet.

Union...

When I was no longer useful, you decided to neglect me;
You were done, saying you needed to be free:
The feelings I had for you, were loyal and true;
But you still abandoned me, saying "out with the old, and
in with the new,"
Now I got a different perspective, with a wiser objective;
As of now, I'm very selective:
My heart is sensitive, and it needs to be protected:
You made it hard for me to love, or trust another;
I thought you were my soulmate, much more than a lover:
You had me fooled for so very, very long;
But now I'm past your deception, and standing strong:
So, I thank you because I'm also free;
To carefully select someone, who's right for me:
Someone who'll have my back, and will be in my corner:
That'll be loyal to me because they're my partner:
I'm on my own, destined to have great things;
To pair up with someone suitable,
who knows I'm worthy to wear his ring:
I need someone who appreciates the gift, to truly be loved;
To be cherished, lavished, and adored me, like the purity of a dove:
Who'll understand all my worth;
Under no circumstances, will he ever desert:
Continued On Next Page

He calls me his beautiful, sensation-able Queen;
Who's luxurious and radiates passion, suitable for her King:
His love for me will fill my soul with enough energy
to send a jet soaring through space;
His compassion will be humble enough,
where I'll always respect my place:
His honor will be to our Lord and Savior Jesus Christ first;
Then he can love me like God loves the church:
There's no doubt this time, I'll be waiting on the man
that's meant for me;
And God will bless our union in holy matrimony.

Issues...

You're so old, fat, and disgusting;
You're not respected or even trusted:
Always tired I think you're lazy;
Always cursing and talking crazy:
Sitting around with anger and grief;
Get up, get out, and get some relief:
You complain about your body being weak, and always hurting;
You need to move around and exercise, and that's for certain:
You're just comfortable doing nothing at all;
You don't even sit up to take a call:
Stop lying around on the phone;
Go outside get out your comfort zone:
I know your legs hurt from having gout;
But you in that house day in and day out:
It's a whole world out there just waiting on you;
I'm sure you can find something you like to do:
Take a walk or go to school;
Buy a paper, read the news:
Join a club or volunteer;
Do something useful, snap into gear:
Sitting around just wasting time;
It ain't good for your body or your mind:
Eating all that junk, and unhealthy food;
No wonder you keep an attitude:
Continued On Next Page

What you're doing isn't okay, and it ain't fine;
Life isn't forever- you run out of time:
You can walk, run, even jump;
Just get yourself together, and get out of that slump;
Get rid of the bitterness and the strife.
Cause today is the first day of the rest of your life!

Tripping...

Man, ain't nobody tripping off you but you;
You always think somebody's worried about
the way you look, or what you said;
You so conceited, it's gone to your head:
You always trying to dress, in the latest fashion;
You don't have any real style, and you lack passion:
You always jumping, to the worst conclusion;
You're just paranoid, and filled with illusion:
You need to go ahead on, with that junk, and
find something else to do;
Cause ain't nobody tripping off that junk, but you.
Everywhere you go, you think all eyes on you;
No, no, no, people have better things to do!
You're so confrontational, and filled with grief;
Everyone is not out to get you, regardless of your belief:
You're so bitter, and filled with pain;
I'm surprised your own insecurities, haven't driven you insane:
The stuff you worry about is pretty, ludicrous;
Let your guard's down and live, take some risk:
When you look in the mirror, what exactly did you see?
A man on the other side, begging for you to set him free:
Go on and live your life, for Heaven's sake;
It won't be perfect; you'll make some mistakes:
Stop tripping off what people say or do;
Continued On Next Page

On the contrary, they're not worried about you:
Step out your shell, and take a chance;
You might even enjoy life, and find romance:
We all run into a situation or two;
Just deal with it, and push on through:
Cause ain't nobody tripping off you but you!
Life is too complicated always to have an attitude;
Walking around obnoxious, and always being rude:
You got a chip on your shoulder, thinking life owes you something;
Get out of your own way, before you end up with nothing:
You don't know what you want, but you want it to be known;
So, you jock people's style, and call it your own:
You need to find your 'niche,' and find it fast;
Because life goes on-but yours won't last:
Live a little bit, "make it do what it do,"
Cause ain't nobody tripping off for you but you!

What...

I don't condone your promiscuous behavior;
But I had some thoughts, that would've worked in your favor:
The child you're carrying is innocent to all;
But you shut me out, so my back is against the wall;
I would've done whatever it took to help you out;
I'm loyal as they come, and that's no doubt:
I tried to show sympathy and a little pity;
But you want to be bougie and high saditty:
So, I'm going to back up off, all the above;
Leaving you and your baby, a whole lot of love:
We're family, and I was trying to be helpful;
But some of your actions, are very disrespectful:
You refuse to compromise, so why even bother;
But you had no demands, to put on the baby's father:
You need to seriously think about the decisions, that you make;
Before you end up alone with a hollering baby, and a big headache:
You don't have to listen, or even take my advice;
You're a grown woman, and it's your life:
I'm sure with your best efforts; you can get it together:
I'm going to leave it alone, and let you do better:
There are no hard feelings, and no love lost;
You just save me a whole lot of time, and spared me the cost:
So, when he comes into this world, I'll meet your son;
Because right about now, girl, I'm done!

Betrayal...

Accepting everything someone does and says;
And never even challenging, their wicked ways:
Suspecting in your heart, they might be a liar;
However, you weren't brave enough, to dismiss or fire:
Carrying this burden, on your shoulder;
It gets heavier, as it gets older:
Now you're loyal, all the time;
But not a shred of honesty, did you find:
You walk around pretending, all is well;
Too embarrassed to even tell:
Things get worse, by the day;
But you fooled everyone, into thinking it's okay:
You'll pay the price when things go wrong;
And you're left to deal with it, on your own:
When you're sure that things aren't right;
It makes you want to fuss, and fight:
You're wound up tight, from bad decisions;
You can't ignore it, cause it's your business:
A lying friend will make you stop, and pause;
You'll never drop your guards, or trust at all:
Now, this betrayal has hardened, your heart;
So, you keep your distance, which is smart:
You're determined never to trust again;
Because you were betrayed by a friend.

Confusion...

You're trapped in an illusion;
With a lot of confusion:
In your mind you try to escape;
Avoiding nonsense is not a debate:
You want desperately, not to participate;
In all the things you despise and hate:
In certain situations; you won't understand;
When high order of truths, or in demand:
Things of deception seem to be unclear;
Losing face is your biggest fear:
Deception had you in its hold;
You try to stay focus, but you're out of control:
With all the lies, you don't want to trip,
But you're caught in a triangle, and losing your grip:
Now you're aggravated, and feeling low;
Cause trouble seems to follow you, wherever you go:
You don't want to be bothered, or caught up in a mess;
But the "ball of confusion," won't let you rest:
So, you try to stay subtle, and play by the rules;
But you get overwhelmed, cause you're all confused.

Jealously...

Being envious of someone else's success;
Will keep you miserable, and in distress:
You don't have to degrade others, to be complete;
We're all different, that's what makes us unique:
Be mindful of the things, that you say and do;
Cause people around you, have feelings too:
When you find those with wealth and riches, there's no need for
you to covet;
It's just not your turn to prosper yet:
Don't hate on others, because of their accomplishments;
And have a bitter heart, filled with resentment:
You may be selfish, and don't care;
But being jealous will get you nowhere:
Be content with what you have to give;
And a peaceful and healthier life, you'll live.

Oh Baby...

Oh, sweet baby, don't you cry;
Your Mother wasn't there, but I don't know why.
I know you needed her to comfort you;
In your rough time she didn't see you through:
I know you don't quite understand why she was so hard
and made so many demands:
I know you had a pretty rough childhood;
You didn't laugh and play as much as you could;
She put you through some unnecessary stuff;
She made it hard; she made it rough:
She denied you of a simple life; she needs to make amends and
sacrifice:
After the tears and pain, it still won't matter;
I know that's your mother, and you'll love her forever:

But now she has a part of you;
That's your daughter, don't let her ruin her too:
It's time to fight child;
And do it right away, God will bless you for it one day:
If you sit back and don't do anything;
God will curse you,
Find your strength in Jesus and be bold;
Mother your daughter; take some controls:
Continued On Next Page

I know it's going to take hard work to get it all done;
It's not going to be easy, and it's not going to be fun:
It'll take some adjusting and a whole lot of changes;
But she's your daughter, not a stranger.

I'll be there for you when you need me; there's no doubt;
I know I'm not your mother, but I am your Aunt!
Oh, sweet baby, don't you sigh;
Hold on to my love, and don't you cry.

Missed guided affection Part 1

Missed guided affection;
Only faith in Jesus can reunite the connection:
I need you to acknowledge me;
Patient and understanding is the key:
In order to live a complete life;
We both need to make a sacrifice:
Let's stop trying to compete, with one another;
We're equally special because we share the same mother:
I'm not perfect, and you're definitely not;
Accepting each other's flaws is what it's really about:
Sometimes we're uneased with each other,
and this goes on for a while:
But when we learn to respect each other,
we'll complement each other's style:
I know I'm older, and should know more
because I've been here longer;
However, you're smart as well, and maybe a bit stronger:
Instead of walking around holding a grudge;
We need to express, our sisterly love:
When I'm hurting, I keep my distance;
But you "nick pick," and taunt at me, and become persistent:
Sometimes you may unintentionally provoke me;
Which brings about my insecurity;
Continued On Next Page

I don't want to fight anymore; it's breaking my heart,
and keeping me sore!
I'm willing to listen if you willing to hear:
All this pain stems, from yesteryears:
I want to end our tears and sorrows;
Let's make brighter days, for our tomorrows:
This isn't about us anymore;
We have kids, and family that sees our scars:
I refuse to waste any more precious time;
Missing you is constantly on my mind:
I'll go first, and apologize;
I hope you follow my lead when you realize:
Since I'm the oldest, all I ever wanted was to be the leader;
To have my little sister because I really need her!

Missedguided affection Part 2..

Of course, I accept your apology;
But now I need for you, to understand me;
My life wasn't always glamorous; I had to go through trials and
take some risk;
Yeah, I may taunt, and tease, and aggravate you;
But I am the little sister, that's what I do!
Stop always trying to outthink me;
I have my own thoughts; can't you clearly see?
It'll make me stop wanting to challenge you;

I'll accept your advice, and listen to:
I may not do everything you say;
But, at least I'll have your views to consider one day:
I agree, a lot of our pain, is still from yesterday;
But we can't live through our past;

We must embrace today:
We must build each other up, to stay strong;
You can't just walk away, and leave me alone!
I refuse to let this stuff linger, and become sad;
I'm not going to waste all my time, staying mad:
I heard you loud and clear, and I know you're right;
I'm on your side big sister, and I don't want to fight:
Continued On Next Page

Yeah, we share the same mother and father too;
That's why I'm willing to put aside our differences and focus on
loving you,
Now please accept my apology;
I need my big sister, can't you see.

Chapter 5

Entertainment

1. Open mic
2. Print this
3. Nothin Comin
4. The Movement
5. Out there
6. Beautiful Sky
7. Stinky
8. The Neighbor
9. I write
10. Do it
11. Wild Stallion

Open Mic...

I came out tonight, and it was on point;
It was all good vibes, right from the start:
I was like a kid in a candy store, just wanting more;
Or an astronaut traveling through space needing to explore:
I was spitting some poems, and others were too;
They sounded like, some spirits that I knew:
All the talent that was on the mic;
Kept me entertained, the whole night:
The friend I came with had to leave a little early;
She left me by myself, but I wasn't worried:
I was in good company- didn't she know;
There's no way I was going to miss that show:
My friend didn't stay; it was her lost;
I had to tell afterward, how we rocked the house.
When I looked around the scenery;
I must admit, it was all new to me:

We came together in unity;
Encouraging each other, it was a sight to see:
Didn't anybody put up a fuss or fight;
Everybody there, respect the mic:
A lot of them there were young enough, to be my kids;
But when I got on that mic, I fit right in;
They rapped, sang, and dance like it was no tomorrow;
Continued On Next Page

Some shared poems of the time, others shared their sorrows,
And I'm definitely coming back, to do it again;
Because while I was out, I met a lot of friends:
I know what it's like to be truly free;
And bear your soul to the people you meet:
I had so much fun at 'open mic';
Just listening and cheering throughout the night.
I got up and shared a poem I'd written myself;
The audience cheered, as their hearts melt:
I'm coming back again, every Friday night;
Cause, I can't resist that open mic!

Print This...

Office Depot is the store I go to print out my poems and a whole
lot more;
I made a lot of friends over time;
Just by sharing stories and sharing rhymes:
They're all equally special to me;
And my smile lights up the room you see:
One of the managers always discounts my purchases;
Keeping me satisfied for certain:
One particular employee finds me all the sale items;
Which makes my day a little brighter.
Another employee helps me with any and everything
and all the above;
And in return, I feed him and call him my son:
One young lady reads and helps edit my work;
And she's the sweetest ever counter clerk:
This one manager he's so cool;
He said when he meets his store quantum
he'll dress like an afro dude:
There's also a cashier who's so nice;
She works at another area job, so I get to greet her twice:
One of the employees went to school with my son;
When I bring my son along they reminisce about their past fun:
I'm trying to get them to put me on their payroll;
I made a special greeting for the customers
Continued On Next Page

to get their merchandise sold:
I won't dare get my computer at home fixed;
Cause all this fun I refuse to miss:
I'm sure that they enjoy my presence as well;
Through their smiles, I can definitely tell.

Nothin Comin...

You slipped, I tripped;
Now you wanna, give me lip:
What's to say? There's nothing left:
Just quit playing with yourself:
You trying to be hip, and run some game;
Don't you know you're sounding lame;
Did you think it was going to work?
I already know you're a fake jerk:
What are you reading, a player's book?
It's "Players for Dummies," you need to look!
Get a life, and do it fast;
Cause the stuff you're doing ain't go last:
You slipped up and messed around;
Now you are looking like a clown:
You can't just go back in time;
The life I save will be mine:
You're ratchet, trifling, and very low;
And you wanna date me? -"I don't think so!"
Your sorry butt, ain't got nothin comin;
I'm about to leave and, take off running:
To all men, you're a big disgrace;
So, let's keep it real, and get on out my face:
What, you looking for somebody to lay up on?
Continued On Next Page

Get a job, and get a place of your own:
And if you're trying to make a commitment;
Then you need to know; I ain't with it;
I know what, your sorry butt is really about;
And true leopards never change their spots:
I don't know why you keep trying to holla at me;
U ain't got nothin comin, you lame creep.

The Movement...

You need to release; it needs to come out;
By all means necessary, without a doubt:
Let it out and do it fast;
Stop sitting around passing gas:
It's making a noise, and smelling loud;
Get that waist out your bowels:
It'll make your stomach twist around;
Until that junk come on down:
If it doesn't come, you're in lots of pain;
Without the movement, you'll go insane:
It's no secret; it's no shame;
We all must go, we're all the same:
When it's solid it's hard to come;
But when it's loose, you better run:
If you wait by stalling time,
Your pants will end up filled with slime.
It won't be nice if you poop your pants;
That first warning is your only chance:
Now you're wondering what to do;
When all that poop is covering you:
All your friends will leave real quick;
Cause they don't wanna smell that stitch:
Continued On Next Page

So, don't wait until it hit the floor;
And you knew you had to go:
You tried to say; it was a little gas;
No-you needs to wash your ash:
When you get too old, and moving slow;
Then wear diapers when you need to go:
If your bowels won't work and you need a bag;
That's okay; it's out your ash:
The food tastes good going down;
But when it's coming out, it smells loud:
Now you don't need to make an excuse;
Just go sit down and take a poop!
It's okay, just go on and spray;
Get that smell out for the day.

Out there

I met some new friends tonight, some of which knew the light;
Even on a drunken high, they were able to testify:
As I sat there for a while,
One of them tried to jock my style:
I wasn't worried not a bit, even though I couldn't "spit:"
They all gather around in their chairs; for a poem, I wanted to
share;
A man shouted, "if u can't spit it, you must don't know it;"
I read what I wrote- I guess I blew it:
If I memorize everything I write;
I'll be up all night for the rest of my life:
I know my work, and I know it's good;
The gift I got, wasn't understood:
I'm sure I made a good impression;
Cause I came with a positive message:
I'm glad I came out to mingle;
The crowd was great with a Christmas jingle:
One lady made me laugh and want to jump;
Because every song they play she got up and stomped:
She even told me to stop that laughing and talking. Before she put
me out, and I will end up walking:
I had a good time, and that's all that matters;
In spite of the cold, in spite of the weather:
Continued On Next Page

68

I saw my girlfriend I hadn't seen in years;
All the things life took us through we held back the tears:
We wished we had a been there more for each other;
We both had husbands and even lovers:
We reconnected, and that's what really counts;
Our friendship is strong, and that's no doubt:
We had so many things to catch up on;
Stories to share about the unknown:
We blocked out everyone in the room to get a little gossip in;
I had to scream over the music, just to talk to my friend:
We haven't been in each other lives we've just been neutral;
I've missed her a lot, and I'm sure the feeling is mutual:
I didn't really want the night to end;
It could've gone on forever, cause I was with my friend:
I hope we get together again real soon;
Day or night or even afternoon.

Beautiful Sky...

Look at the beautiful sky, the clouds rippling so high, They're con-
stantly on the move;
Even though you're passing by:
Wanting to stay, and capture its sites;
Needing to be gone, before the night:
Watching the moon come rushing through;
Knowing her peace is soothing to you:
Seem to enjoy the stars above:
As the universe share, it's love:
Always knowing the right words to say;
A romantic couple, getaway:
Calm is the evening, gentle sky;
Enjoying the beauty, from the life's that fly:
Staying all night, until the sunrise;
Admiring the sparkles, in your eyes:
It's always a pleasure, to do it again;
And watch the beautiful sky, with a friend:
If you need to be fulfilled;
Watch the sky change, it's a thrill;
She'll turn dark, in the middle of the day;
To let you know a storm, is on the way;
She'll stay bright, to the early night;
Helping us out, by extending her light:
Continued On Next Page

When she loses her light, in the late afternoon;
We know 'day-light-savings,' is coming soon:
I'll always enjoy her beautiful shine;
As a reflection of life, from yours to mine:
So next time when you are passing by;
Take the time to admire the beautiful sky.

Stinky...

I don't want to be a stinky bucket;
Please don't let me be funky:
The 'power' went out, in the frost;
But I still had to wash the dirt off:
I'll bathe by candlelight;
I need to be clean through the night:
I can't go around smelling bad;
It makes me sick, and it makes me mad:
I can't have nobody asking, "what's that smell?"
It's so foul; they wanted to yell!
From that nasty annoying smell:
So, if I were you, I'd keep it clean;
Cause I'll tell you if you stink and be real mean:
I can't tolerate really bad odors;
Smelling like a bum or nasty hoarder:
You can use my water, and I'll buy you some soap;
Cause unpleasant smells, make me choke:
So, don't go around being a stinky bucket;
Being all nasty smelling funky:
So, wash it, wash it, if you will;
Scrub it high, scrub It low, scrub where no one dares to go:
I'll keep it clean, and make it shine;
And make sure that funk is yours, not mine:
Keep it clean, keep it sweet;
Continued On Next Page

Make sure that smell, is not your feet:
Wash it up, clean the mess;
Make sure you keep your body fresh:
Wash the bottom, wash the top;
Don't just smell like a dirty mop:
Make sure you get the smell all out;
Cause if you don't, I'm going to shout:
Take a bath, or take a shower;
Make sure it's clean, within an hour:
Wipe and scrub the dirt in the tub;
Wash that funk down, and you rub, rub, rub:
Wash it up, suds that rag;
Make sure you clean, your nasty ash:
Nobody wants to smell your dusty butt;
So, don't forget to wash it up!

The Neighbor...

They're always there, trying to do you a favor;
They live close by; it's your neighbor:
They'll always borrow some sugar from you;
And a whole lot more, that's what they do:
If you have a dog that's supposed to be a watch guard;
They'll let you know when it's out the yard;
They stare out the window when they're bored;
But when they want your attention, they're not to be ignored:
They know everybody's business, on the block;
They can tell you, if your front door is opened, or locked:
They'll give you a ride when you're without a car;
They'll watch your kids, and steal your heart:
They'll stay up with you, all night long;
Just listening to music or playing cards.

Some of them are very annoying;
So, you try to play it off like you're not into partying:
But when they see other's cars in your driveway;
They come and knock on your door, anyway:
Now you're stuck having to let them in;
Hoping they don't embarrass you in front of your friends:
They play cool like they came to borrow some eggs;
And invite themselves to stay, just to get in your head:
Continued On Next Page

Now you're all worked up, cause they got under your skin;
And you think to yourself, why in the hell did I let him in:
Now you put everybody out, saying you're going to call it a night;
But your neighbor's drunk in the driveway, trying to start a fight:
Your neighbor comes over the next day trying to apologize;
With a case of beer, and a baked surprise:
Now you know that you just can't up and move;
So, you swallow your pride, and deal with the fool:
One thing for sure, you'll have to learn;
You don't want to cross the neighbors, are be on bad terms:
If things go south, you won't know who to tell;
Cause the wrong neighbor, can make your life a living hell!
But with the right neighbor, you'll get along well.

I Write...

I write poems effortlessly
In order for shut eyes to see;
I write poems, on demand;
Some are informative, inspirational,
loving, or of sorrow because I can.
Some are spiritual or special dedication;
Some of them are entertaining, others are educational:
I write to soothe the soul, in distress;
I write from my heart; I give it my best:
I write for a response from the audience, it's meant;
I write until my heart is filled, with content;
I write when I'm tired and have nothing to show;
I write when I'm busy, and even on the go:
I write when I'm inspired, happy, or sad;
I write when I'm curious, excited, or mad:
I write what I mean, and I write what I feel;
I write messages that are so powerful, they give me a thrill:
I write about people, and I write about things;
I'll write spiritual awareness, and I write songs to sing:
I write through barrels that people refuse, to discuss;
I write about the shame, the pain, and our faith we trust:
I write about the stuff you'll choose, to read over again;
I write about things; you'll share with a friend:
Continued On Next Page

I write when I'm sick, and I write, when I'm well;
I write about things that I need to tell:
I write poems, about writing about poems;
I write poems with laughter, and with charm:
I write when I should sleep, and when I should eat;
I write at the beginning, and at the end of the week:
I write about people, who're anxious and depressed;
I write kind words, to give them faith, to be blessed:
When I write poems, all my feelings; I release;
The satisfaction through writing brings me joy and peace.

Do it...

Lifted, lifted, lift it high;
Lift, it till it touches the sky;
Sing it, sing it, sing it loud;
Sing it till it's heard in a crowd:
Pray for it, pray for it, pray it hard;
Pray it till it's heard by the Lord:
Shake it, shake it, shake it well;
Shake it to it make you yell:
Roll it, roll it, roll it down;
Roll it to it, hit the ground:
Grab it, grab it, grab it hard:
Grab to you wanna start:
Pull it, pull it, pull it tight;
Pull it till is out of sight:
Stomp it, stump it, stomp it fast;
Stump till it break the glass:
Wipe it, wipe it, wipe it clean;
Wipe it till it makes you scream:
Brush, it, brush it, brush it out;
Brush, it til it makes you shout:
Wear it, wear it, wear it well;
Wear it till you're looking swell:
Hold it, hold it, hold it tight;
hold it til you see the light:
Continued On Next Page

Eat it, eat it, eat it all;
Eat until you start to fall;
Tell it, tell it, tell it right;
Tell it till you wanna fight:
Play it, play it, play it fun;
Play it til you need to run
Watch it, watch it, watch it close;
Watch it til you see the most:
Hear it, hear it, hear it clear;
Hear til you hear it near:
Stir it, stir it, stir it smooth;
Stir until you get your groove:
Find it, find it, find it fast;
Find it til you find some cash:
Know it, know it, know it well;
Know it till you need to tell:
Spit it, spit it, spit it out;
Spit it til it's out your mouth:
Learn it, learn it, learn it smart;
Learn it til you know your part:
Read it, read it, read it loud;
Read it til it makes you proud:
Do it, do it, do it good;
Do it like you knew you could.

Wild Stallion...

I'm a wild stallion that can't be tamed;
If you even attempt it, I'll put you to shame:
Everybody I meet wanna run some game;
They must don't know, the story behind my name:
I'm hip as they come and smooth as can be:
That's why all the 'players,' trying to holler at me:
I ain't got time to give them all a turn;
So, I sit back and laugh, and watch them squirm:
I'm free as a bird, flying high in the sky;
I'll never settle down, so don't ask me why:
I go here and there, from place to place;
I got so much going on; it keeps a smile on my face:
You can hook up with me, or not, but it won't last long;
I'm a wild stallion, that has to roam:
I hope you're not sensitive, cause you'll get your feelings hurt;
I'm not trying to be loyal; I just like to flirt:
I'm just passing through, with a lot of the delight;
I'll be on to the next, before the end of the night:
Believe me when I tell you, that you don't want to be none;
But, I'll hook up with you,
just for the fun:
Continued On Next Page

I have no idea what a commitment means;
I'm trying to "get some ghost", and leave the scene:
I'm a wild stallion, that can't be tamed;
The name might change, but the game remains:
If you try to follow me, you'll be left behind;
I'll run fast as the wind, and I'm hard to find:
If you think you're compatible, and on my level;
Hang if you can, but it won't last forever:
I don't answer to no one I meet;
I move so fast; the wind can't catch my feet:
You can admire my beauty, with a quick glance;
However, I'm not available, for long romance:
I don't want a relationship, so let's keep things clear;
I'm a wild stallion, free-spirited,
You hear!

Chapter 6

Special Dedication

1. T. D.
2. Baby Boy
3. The Message
4. Faith
5. Blessed
6. Praise God
7. Loyal Days
8. Comfort

T.D...

I was born with the stigma of being a lefty;
But with these hands I'm talented and very crafty:
I was talked about from having dark skin;
From strangers to family to even friends:
No one cared or knew; they didn't see my pain;
So, I kept it inside and hid my shame:

While in grade school I did my part;
I wasn't top of the class or even that smart:
I did my best, so they passed me alone;
I completed a trade; now I'm standing strong:
I became a mother and a wife;
But God had a special calling, on my life:
I talk to young people in society;
Because I'm saved and sanctify, I'm a missionary:
I minister to a lot of people, I speak to the crowd;
I bear witness of God's glory, and I say it out loud!
I still work a full-time job;
But my best rewards are being God's child:
I'm waiting on all my children, to come on in;
To trust in Jesus to be their Savior and their friend:
I want my whole family; I want the world to know;
That Jesus is the light and the way to go:
Continued On Next Page

In the Bible God often made references, through numbers;
And I was the third child, born to my mother:
In John 1:17 Jonah stayed in the whale's belly for three days;
We need the Father the Son, and the Holy Spirit, to be saved:
There are 27 books in the New Testament
$3 \times 3 \times 3$ three to the third power:
Jesus prayed three times in the Garden of Gethsemane,
before his arrest;
Christ was placed on the cross, on the third hour 9 a.m.,
and he died on the 9th hour 3 p.m.
He lay dead for three days and three nights.
It was only three witnesses to Jesus resurrection John,
Peter, and James.
In Daniel 3:23-25 there were three men in the fiery furnace, and it
took me three years of studying to learn this:
I'm the third child, number 3 for a reason;
It's time to reap God's rewards; it's my season.

Baby Boy...

You were just an infant so innocent and pure;
I'll always be your mother, and that's for sure:
You didn't come from my body, but that's okay;
Cause I love you with all my heart anyway:
With those little tiny hands and those little tiny feet;
You didn't take up much space and didn't need much to eat:
When I first laid eyes on you it was love at first sight;
I didn't hesitate or put up a fight:
You were so easy to love all cuddly and cute;
Looking so adorable in your newborn suit:
I already had a house full of children waiting to love you as well;
The way they passed you around from arm to arm
I could definitely tell:
We welcomed you into our home making you part of the family;
And when you needed a mama you looked up to me:
You played and laughed all the time and was so full of life;
That alone made me happy to be your dad's wife:
Your birth mom was sick and couldn't take care of you;
So, she gave you to me, and I knew exactly what to do;
With your little bitty self-touched all our hearts;
And each one of us did our part:
We kept you happy and satisfied;
Loving and nurturing
so, you could survive:
Continued On Next Page

One day your daddy decided to leave, and he took you with him;
We were all heartbroken and filled with grim:
I thought about you each-and-every day,
praying that you were all right;
Loving you, even more, when you are out of my site:
One day I got a knock at my door, and it was you;
Your dad had a change of heart from whatever
life took him through:
My heart was overwhelmed and filled with joy;
When I open my front door, and saw my little boy:
I hope we stay connected for the rest of your life;
So, I can watch you grow up and become
a man and one day take a wife:
As of now, I cherish all the moments we spend;
Cause I am your mother and your friend.

The Message...

The message at church came with lots of love;
He spoke about our Father from above:
His words were all heaven-sent;
After listening our hearts were very content:
This man was very blessed indeed;
Exactly what the congregation, needs:
I'm glad I didn't miss church today;
The preacher's words won't fade away:
He laid hands of faith on everyone in the room;
Assuring them that their blessings were coming soon:
He spoke of God as being our Father;
How we can call on our Daddy at any hour:
I was filled with joy after hearing his sermon;
The message was powerful with discernment:
We're in revival all this week;
To hear him speak again will be a treat:
His wife is also a woman of God;
They both have words to anoint the crowd:
Make sure you come out for all this love:
He'll teach you about mercy from our Father above:
Their messages together will change your life;
May God continue to bless both him and his wife.
Dedicated to: Elder Darnell

Faith...

It's just nice to be nice, and I'm glad you are to me;
Because I know in my heart you are a sweetie:
Some things over time made you a little tart;
But when they dissolved you became a sweetheart:
Sometimes life takes us through bitter pain;
And when it's over we don't remain the same:
I know your pride has been bruised and you have
a lot of hidden scars;
Stop me if you will if I've gone too far;
Secrets are not meant to stay in the past;
Sometimes we dig them up, so our future doesn't crash:
And you must remember God takes out the trash:
So, if they're still bothering you and you must repent;
Go ahead it's okay cause God forgives and forgets:
You're a new creature born through Christ each day;
A total transformation when it's done his way:
People will prosecute you again, and again:
They'll continue to bring up your past when you use to sin;
That's alright because God is with you, and you have his peace;
You'll feel it more and more as your faith increase;
So, go on and cry, now dry your eyes;
You'll be blessed, and they'll wonder why:
Your cup will run over, and that's for sure;
Continued On Next Page

From all the things you had to endure:
So, find your strength and find it fast;
Because hard times will never last:
What God has for you, it is for you;
Regardless of what anyone says or do:
God will keep you safe in his arms;
Where no one can do you any harm:
So, keep your faith until you die;
Our Father will be waiting beyond the sky:
Dedicated to:
Felicia

Blessed...

It's a man in our congregation;
He inspires all our generations:
He's a church Elder and a minister too;
He also preaches God's good news:
He's the music teacher at the school;
Who sings the Gospel, not the blues.
After you hear his words you are inspired;
He's a humble man to admire:
He's always helping here and there;
Extending generosity everywhere:
It's an honor if you meet his presence;
Even if it's just for singing lessons:
If singing is your true desire;
Then follow him he directs the choir:
His voice is like Heaven-sent;
He praises God with content:
And when he preaches it's a big delight;
He brings God word to the light:
The way he preaches will make you moan;
And you're bound to get your praises on:
The man I speak of is my brother through Christ;
May God continue to bless him throughout his life:
Dedicated to: Elder Andrew

Praise God...

One of the saints at church had a situation
that was bothering her a bit;
She responded by saying that she's going to put 'a praise on it':
She's waiting on little-old-me to write a poem for her;
I'm truly honored just to share:
This lady is really wonderful indeed;
She'll show you how to praise God, for what you need:
The lady I'm referring to is so sweet;
She took time out, to come to my grandmother's 'Home Going
Service,' just to speak:
When she gives God the glory, and get her praise on;
If you sit still, you're on your own:
She makes everyone in the room, wanna jump and shout;
She really shows you what praising the Lord, is all about:
When I hugged her, I felt a spiritual energy and a lot of love;
She's truly anointed from our Father above:
She had something troubling her at home;
However, she testified with a song:
It was so special to see the relief on her face;
When she testified how God delivered her, through his Grace:
It's a glorious feeling to have such an anointed sister, through
Christ;
Just meeting her presence enriches my life:
She's an evangelist also, and oh how she delivers God's word;
Continued On Next Page

Unlike any woman I've ever heard:
And she kept her peace throughout God's test;
It's a perfect reflection on how she's truly blessed:
I would like to let you know that the pleasure is all mine;
To stand before everyone and read her poem this time:
Dedicated to: Evangelist White

Loyal Days...

Through Christ we're all sisters and brothers;
However, she's one of our own loyal Church Mother's:
She's very humble and soft-spoken;
She's one of God's saints, not easily broken:
She's a gentle spirit, that's welcoming when you're near;
She always responds by showing she cares:
She doesn't talk much.
However, the words she does say;
Will keep you uplifted throughout your day:
When I see her at church, it's definitely a pleasure;
The peace around her evolves into no measure:
She's been here all along;
when her late husband's ministry ran this place;
She stays on to help guide us, through God's grace:
I want her to know that we appreciate all the sacrifices she's made;
Her contributions and dedications will never fade:
She's sitting in the front pew, all elegant with class;
God has blessed her with favor from her past:
She's covered with the blood of Jesus
for whatever she goes through;
Continued On Next Page

She knows God's amazing grace, and his mercy too:
When you stop and pay attention, it's easy to recognize;
Mother Thompson is filled with the Holy Spirit,
and she's Sanctified:
May God continue to bless her, throughout her days;
And allow her to live them out peacefully, from her loyal ways:
Dedicated to: Mother Thompson

Comfort...

David was a father, son, brother, cousin, and a friend;
None of us wanted his life to end:
'We're all saddened when someone we love dies;
We believe that God is waiting for them beyond the sky:
The sun is shining, for God has called one of his angels home;
He was weary, and his suffering was long:
Death is a very natural part of life;
Yet, our hearts are still broken.
However, we must accept it, after the fight:
But, you're not in this fight alone;
Trust that he's now in the comfort of Jesus' arms:
We'll all remember him by his beautiful smile;
We'll save the image in our hearts for a while:
We'll miss him dearly, and that's for sure;
But he was tired from the things he endured:
His body was sick and needed to rest;
He's home with Our Lord and Savior; he's truly blessed:

You'll mourn today, and cry on through tomorrow;
May the love of Jesus comfort you through your sorrows:
God will give you peace in the midst of your storm;
Just knowing that this world can no longer do David any harm:
His time here on earth was done and satisfy;
Continued On Next Page

His place of rest was not denied:
His suffering is over, and the pain is at ease:
God said, "Well done my fair child" cause he was pleased:
Now we all need to dry our eyes;
For, we shall see David again on the other side.

On February 6, 2017, David was given his wings,
from Our Father above;
He'll be greatly missed because he was truly loved.
Dedicated to: David (3-24-44) to (2-6-17)

X

CPSIA information can be obtained
at www.ICGtesting.com
Printed in the USA
FFHW01n1449300818
48053056-51767FF